5

Let's go by Car

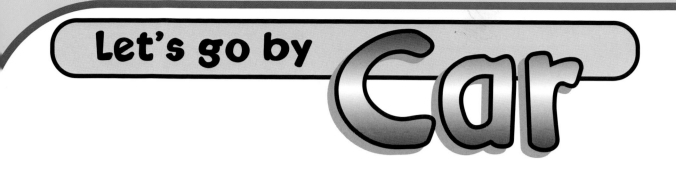

Barbara Hunter

Heinemann
LIBRARY

Little Nippers

H **www.heinemann.co.uk/library**
Visit our website to find out more information about **Heinemann Library** books.

To order:
☎ Phone 44 (0) 1865 888066
▤ Send a fax to 44 (0) 1865 314091
▢ Visit the Heinemann Bookshop at www.heinemann.co.uk/library to browse our catalogue and order online.

First published in Great Britain by Heinemann Library, Halley Court, Jordan Hill, Oxford OX2 8EJ, part of Harcourt Education.
Heinemann is a registered trademark of Harcourt Education Ltd.

Editorial: Jilly Attwood and Claire Throp
Design: Jo Hinton-Malivoire and bigtop, Bicester, UK
Models made by: Jo Brooker
Picture Research: Lodestone Publishing Limited
Production: Lorraine Warner

Originated by Dot Gradations
Printed and bound in China by South China Printing Company

ISBN 0 431 16463 0 (hardback)
06 05 04 03 02
10 9 8 7 6 5 4 3 2 1

ISBN 0 431 16468 1 (paperback)
06 05 04 03 02
10 9 8 7 6 5 4 3 2 1

British Library Cataloguing in Publication Data
Hunter, Barbara
Let's go by car
388.3'2
A full catalogue record for this book is available from the British Library.

Acknowledgements
The publishers would like to thank the following for permission to reproduce photographs:
Alvey and Towers pp. **6**, **16**, **18**, **19**; Bubbles p. **7a** (Pauline Cutler); Collections p. **15** (Peter Wright); Sally & Richard Greenhill Photo Library p. **10** (Sally Greenhill), p. **20-21** (Richard Greenhill); Sylvia Cordaiy Photo Library p. **17** (Humphrey Evans); Tografox pp. **4-5**, **7b**, **8**, **9**, **11**, **12-13**, **14** (R. D. Battersby).

Cover photograph reproduced with permission of PA Photos (Phil Noble).

The publishers would like to thank Annie Davy for her assistance in the preparation of this book.

Every effort has been made to contact copyright holders of any material reproduced in this book. Any omissions will be rectified in subsequent printings if notice is given to the publishers.

2

Contents

Journeys.. 4

Why do people go by car?............... 6

On the road 8

Driving a car.................................. 10

At the garage................................. 12

Road maps and signs 14

Traffic lights.................................. 16

Parking.. 18

Big cars.. 20

Shapes... 22

Index 24

Journeys

Where did you go on your last car journey?

Where do you think these people are going?

Why do people go by car?

Shopping

Work

Holiday

On the road

Cars drive on the road.

You must always wear your
seatbelt in a car.

Driving a car

Drivers make the car go where they want by using the steering wheel.

They have a horn to let other drivers know they are there.

Honk!

Honk!

At the garage

Drivers must put fuel into a car to make it **go**.

Road maps and signs

Drivers sometimes use a map to find out where they want to go.

Do you know what this sign is?

Traffic lights

Traffic lights show drivers if it is safe for them to go.

Do you know what the green light means?

Parking

Road

Car park

Big cars

Some cars are very, very big.

Have you seen a huge car like this before?

Shapes

What shapes can you see
on a car journey?

wheel